POPE
FRANCIS

Spiritual Leader and Voice of the Poor

POPE
FRANCIS

Spiritual Leader and Voice of the Poor

BY AMANDA LANSER

CONTENT CONSULTANT
DR. MASSIMO FAGGIOLI
ASSISTANT PROFESSOR
HISTORY OF MODERN CHRISTIANITY
UNIVERSITY OF SAINT THOMAS

ABDO
Publishing Company

CREDITS

Published by ABDO Publishing Company, PO Box 398166, Minneapolis, MN 55439.
Copyright © 2014 by Abdo Consulting Group, Inc. International copyrights reserved
in all countries. No part of this book may be reproduced in any form without written
permission from the publisher. The Essential Library™ is a trademark and logo of ABDO
Publishing Company.

Printed in the United States of America,
North Mankato, Minnesota
072013
092013

♻ THIS BOOK CONTAINS AT LEAST 10% RECYCLED MATERIALS.

Editor: Arnold Ringstad
Series Designer: Becky Daum

Photo credits: Tony Gentile/AP Images, cover, 2; Gregorio Borgia/AP Images, 6;
Alessandra Tarantino/AP Images, 10, 58; L'Osservatore Romano/AP Images, 13, 77,
84, 94; Reed Saxon/AP Images, 14; Ivan Fernandez/AP Images, 16; Victor R. Caivano/
AP Images, 20; AP Images, 22; Bettmann/Corbis/AP Images, 26; El Salvador School/
AP Images, 30, 36; North Wind Picture Archives, 33; Gianni Foggia/AP Images, 39;
Eduardo Di Baia/AP Images, 42; Natacha Pisarenko/AP Images, 46; Carlos Barria-La
Nacion/AP Images, 48; Andrew Medichini/AP Images, 52, 74; Massimo Sambucetti/AP
Images, 54; Shutterstock Images, 60; Anton Balazh/Shutterstock Images, 64; Peter Paul
Reubens, 67; Claudio Peri/AP Images, 72; Rigucci/Shutterstock Images, 81; Gretchen
Ertl/AP Images, 87; Luca Bruna/DAPD/AP Images, 91

Library of Congress Control Number: 2013936859

Cataloging-in-Publication Data

Lanser, Amanda.
 Pope Francis: Spiritual leader and voice of the poor / Amanda Lanser.
  p. cm. -- (Essential lives)
ISBN 978-1-61783-704-3
Includes bibliographical references and index.
1. Francis, Pope, 1936- --Juvenile literature. 2. Popes--Biography--Juvenile literature.
I. Title.
282/.092--dc23
[B]   2013936859

CONTENTS

CHAPTER
ONE

FRANCESCO! FRANCESCO!

On a Wednesday evening in early March 2013, Saint Peter's Square in Vatican City was packed with people from all over the world. They had been waiting over a day to see white smoke rising from the chimney of the Sistine Chapel. Four times the crowd had witnessed black smoke coming from the chimney, evidence a new pope had not been elected. Finally, after waiting in the cold rain, tens of thousands of people looked up to see white smoke in the sky.

Cheers of "Habemus Papam!" (We Have a Pope!) erupted across the plaza.[1] People turned their attention to the central balcony of Saint Peter's Basilica. Approximately an hour later, a church official known as a cardinal stepped out onto the balcony. In Latin, Cardinal Tauran exclaimed, "I announce to you a great joy: We have a pope! The eminent and most reverend lord, Lord Jorge, Cardinal of the Holy Roman Church,

The election of Pope Francis surprised and thrilled observers across the globe.

Bergoglio, who has taken for himself the name Francis."[2] The crowd roared and chanted "Francesco! Francesco!" as if to urge the new leader of the Roman Catholic Church to the balcony.[3] At the same time, many Italians in the crowd were shocked and silent. Many had wanted and expected an Italian pope.

The Leader of the Largest Church in the World

The pope is the leader of the Roman Catholic Church, the largest unified religion in the world. There are more than 1 billion Roman Catholics worldwide.[4] The Roman

FRANCIS: A POPE OF FIRSTS

Pope Francis is the first Latin American pope. He was born in Buenos Aires, the capital of Argentina, and he served as the city's archbishop and as the cardinal from Argentina before being elected pope. Latin America is home to 39 percent of the world's 1.1 billion Catholics, a larger proportion than exists in any other part of the world.[5] Many scholars agree the election of a Latin American pope reflects the increasing influence of Latin American Catholics in the Roman Catholic Church.

In addition to being the first Latin American pope, Pope Francis is also the first non-European pope since Syrian pope Gregory III's reign ended in 741 CE. He is also the first pope to come from the Jesuit order of priests, a religious order focusing on education and social justice.

Catholic Church dates back to Jesus and his apostle Peter. According to church tradition, Peter led the church after the crucifixion of Jesus. Since then, the Roman Catholic Church has grown to become one of the most influential organizations in religious history.

Taking on the role of pope is a large responsibility. Not only does the pope lead more than a billion Catholics, but he is also the bishop of Rome and the head of state of Vatican City. This independent nation-state within the city limits of Rome, Italy, is the headquarters of the Roman Catholic Church. The pope nominates cardinals from countries around the world and sets the spiritual tone and vision for the church. When a pope dies, cardinals from all over the world gather in Vatican City to elect a new one. Very rarely, a pope decides to retire rather than serving until his death.

VATICAN CITY

Vatican City, also called simply the Vatican, is an independent nation-state run by the Roman Catholic Church. It is home to Saint Peter's Basilica and Saint Peter's Square. Church tradition says Saint Peter's Basilica was constructed over the tomb of Saint Peter, one of Jesus's 12 disciples. The basilica was originally constructed in the 300s CE during the reign of Roman emperor Constantine I and was then rebuilt during the 1400s and 1500s. It was finally completed in 1626.

The unexpected resignation of Pope Benedict XVI set off a flurry of speculation about the next pope.

The Need for a New Pope

On February 11, 2013, Francis's predecessor, Pope Benedict XVI, sat in a meeting with cardinals at the Vatican. In the middle of the meeting, he announced in Latin, "my strengths, due to an advanced age, are no longer suited" to the job of pope.[6]

When he made the announcement, Pope Benedict XVI was already 85 years old. Though his health was not failing, he was falling victim to the fatigue of age. Some observers noticed he struggled to stay awake during church services. He told the cardinals he would resign on February 28. The announcement came as a surprise not only to the cardinals but also to people all over the world.

Electing a Pope

After Pope Benedict XVI announced his resignation, the

POPE BENEDICT XVI

Formerly known as Cardinal Joseph Ratzinger, Pope Benedict was the first German pope since the 1500s. Pope Benedict XVI was labeled by many as a conservative pope with a masterful knowledge of theology. Though people respected his intellect, he had a difficult time connecting with Catholics whose beliefs sometimes ran counter to official church policies. Pope Benedict was unable to resolve lingering challenges in the church, including the sex abuse scandal and internal issues in the Vatican government.

cardinals set a date to elect a new pope. The selection process is a solemn undertaking steeped in tradition, and voting cardinals take their responsibility extremely seriously. Only cardinals younger than 80 years old may vote. They vote in secrecy during a process called a conclave. The conclave is held in the Vatican's Sistine Chapel. They start the proceedings with a mass in the morning of the first day of the conclave and begin the voting process that afternoon.

One hundred and fifteen cardinals voted in the conclave to elect Pope Benedict XVI's successor. To become elected pope, a candidate—typically a cardinal—must receive at least two-thirds of the votes. The conclave continues until someone wins this majority. It took the cardinals two days and five votes to elect Pope Francis. Compared to others held before the 1900s, it was a quick conclave.

Pope Francis Addresses the World

On the balcony of Saint Peter's Basilica, red curtains parted and Pope Francis stepped forward to greet the expectant crowd below him. Cheers rose up, but people quickly quieted down as he prepared to speak. Camera flashes blinked in the night sky.

Some Catholics hoped Pope Francis would continue Benedict XVI's return to traditionalism. Others believed he would bring reform.

Looking down on the crowd, Pope Francis spoke plainly, clearly, and with humility:

> *You all know that the duty of the conclave was to appoint a bishop to Rome. It seems to me that my brother cardinals have come almost to the ends of the Earth to get him, but here we are. . . . First of all, I would say a prayer: pray for our Bishop Emeritus Benedict XVI.*[7]

Resolving major scandals, including cases of sex abuse by priests, would be a key issue faced by the new pope.

In the days following Pope Francis's election, people across the globe reflected on the challenges he faced as the new leader of the largest Christian church in the world. The Roman Catholic Church had been rocked by scandals in recent years, including accusations of corruption among Vatican City officials and highly publicized sex abuse cases. Some people have criticized the Roman Catholic Church for not embracing modern viewpoints on the role of women in the church, same-sex marriage, and birth control.

Catholics hoped a new direction under a new pope would help the Roman Catholic Church overcome some of these challenges, strengthening the church and attracting more people to the faith. Would Pope Francis be up to the challenge?

THE GREAT WESTERN SCHISM

The last time a pope resigned was in 1415. Between 1378 and 1417, two men claimed to be the leader of the Roman Catholic Church, and each had his own set of followers. This led to a major crisis within the church. Church leaders moved to resolve the schism, or division, by asking the popes to step down and replacing them with a third pope. Though the third pope was elected, neither of the two other popes resigned. Finally, in 1415, the third pope was forced from office, one pope resigned, and the last pope's claim to the papacy was dismissed. This led to the election of Martin V in 1417 and the end of the schism.

CHAPTER
TWO

HUMBLE BEGINNINGS

On December 17, 1936, Mario and Regina Bergoglio of Buenos Aires, Argentina, welcomed a baby boy into the world. Similar to many people in the Flores neighborhood, Mario and Regina were Roman Catholics of Italian descent. The couple named their child Jorge Mario Bergoglio. Seventy-six years later, he would become the world's first Latin American pope.

Flores and Jorge's Buenos Aires

During Jorge's childhood, Flores was a middle-class neighborhood. Most residents were Catholic people of Spanish or Italian heritage. Jorge's mother was the daughter of Italian immigrants, and his father, a railway worker, was born in Italy. Flores was one of dozens of neighborhoods in Buenos Aires, the capital of Argentina.

Jorge Bergoglio was born in his parents' home in Buenos Aires.

Buenos Aires is approximately 150 miles (240 km) from the Atlantic Ocean on the shores of Rio de la Plata.¹ It is one of the most populous and influential Latin American cities. Spanish explorer Pedro de Mendoza founded the city in 1536, 400 years before Jorge was born. The original colony was called Nuestra Señora Santa Mariá del Buen Aire (Our Lady Saint Mary of the Good Air). Due to its river connection to the ocean, Buenos Aires's history as a port city has influenced its character through the years. Many of its residents are immigrants or descendants of immigrants who came to Argentina from Europe by boat.

As with the people of Flores, many residents of Buenos Aires were of European descent. This heritage influenced the city's culture. Today, the city is characterized by the wide avenues and worldly residents more common in Europe than in Latin America. While the city center is home to some entertainment and shopping venues, individual neighborhoods such as Flores are the true hearts of the city. They are where residents meet to discuss politics, celebrate soccer victories, and dance the tango.

Early Passions

Jorge grew up in the midst of this rich culture. He had a love of soccer and tango. Both were popular pastimes in Argentina. He especially loved the tango records of local stars such as Carlos

Gardel and Ada Falcón. Jorge was a popular boy who was friendly and got along easily with his classmates.

When he was 12 years old, Jorge fell in love with a girl in his neighborhood, Amalia, and wrote her a love letter. In it, he promised Amalia he would marry her when they were older and buy her a red and white house. He told Amalia if she would not marry him, he would become a priest. The brief romance was brought to an abrupt end when Amalia's parents forbade her from having contact with Jorge. They thought Amalia was too young to be getting attention from a boy.

TANTALIZING TANGO

The tango is a type of musical style used in ballroom dancing and song. It was first heard in the streets of the lower-class neighborhoods of Buenos Aires in the late 1800s. By the turn of the century, the tango was a popular dance in many different neighborhoods. Gradually, it spread and became a craze in Europe. Tango has its origins in two different dance styles, the Spanish flamenco and the Argentine milonga. It can be lively and fast or slow and melancholy.

As a boy, Jorge was tantalized by the tango. One of his favorite musicians was Carlos Gardel, an artist responsible for popularizing the genre in Argentina and around the world. Before Gardel started writing lyrics to go with tango music, most songs were solely instrumental. A classic example of Gardel's work is "Mi Noche Triste" ("My Sad Night"). The song tells the story of a man longing for a woman who has rejected him.

Amalia, now in her late 70s, still lives in Buenos Aires.

High School Days and a Revelation

As Jorge grew into a young man, he began to take a greater interest in both science and religion. During the school day, Jorge devoted his time to the study of chemistry, spending his mornings working in a lab. At the same time, Jorge's interest in and passion for Roman

Catholicism flourished. Though he was growing into a serious student of the sciences and Catholicism, Jorge also continued to enjoy sports, playing basketball with his friends on his high school's court.

Classmates remember Jorge's devotion to his religion as being intense. His interest would eventually lead to a revelation. During a school break when he was 17, Jorge had an unexpected life-changing experience. One day in September 1954, Jorge went to confession at his local church. He planned to hang out with his friends afterward. However, once he stepped inside the confessional, he was overcome by a spiritual message. As an adult, he would describe the experience as a message from God that "surprised me, with my guard down."[2]

The message was that he was meant to become a priest. For a young man interested in soccer, basketball, and chemistry, it is no wonder the message was surprising. Jorge did not tell anyone about his revelation until he was 21 years old. The revelation would change the course of his life and eventually lead him to Vatican City.

Juan Perón's popular focus on social justice may
have influenced Bergoglio's later beliefs.

Jorge's Argentina

While Jorge was growing up in Buenos Aires, Argentina experienced a period of political unrest. Ten years after his birth, Argentine Army colonel Juan Peròn became president. Previously, Peròn had been the minister of labor in the government, which was controlled by the military.

During his tenure as minister of labor, there was an earthquake in a small town called San Juan. Peròn arranged a fund-raiser for the town, boosting his public image and his popularity. In 1946, Peròn was elected president. His policies focused on the demands of ordinary Argentines, pride of country, and nationalist sentiments. These stances became known as the Peronist movement. The movement is still strong in Argentina today.

After ten years of his presidency, during which the country experienced economic instability, the military overthrew Peròn in 1955 and forced him out of Argentina. He moved from country to country until he returned home in 1973. He remained popular with Argentines and was elected president again that same year. After his death in 1974, his wife, Isabel, took over his administration.

In 1976, the military deposed Isabel in a coup led by Jorge Rafaél Videla. This marked the beginning of a period of internal warfare in Argentina. The political climate while Jorge was growing up and attending college was tumultuous. Things would only get worse in the coming years.

A Brush with Death

In the 1950s, Jorge enrolled in the University of Buenos Aires. He graduated as a chemical technician, but decided later to switch his focus to philosophy and theology. After college, Jorge had a brush with death that strengthened his faith. At the age of 21, he came down with pneumonia, a serious infection of the lungs. Jorge experienced serious complications. His case was so severe doctors had to remove part of his right lung.

Jorge's battle with pneumonia did not make him question his faith. Instead, it increased his devotion to Roman Catholicism. Despite the physical setback, Jorge decided to continue with his spiritual education and growth. On March 11, 1958, he became a prospective member of the Society of Jesus, whose members are known as Jesuits. Jorge was on his way to a future in the Roman Catholic Church.

NOTEWORTHY JESUITS

Pope Francis is not the only notable Jesuit priest. The following men have also made contributions to the Society of Jesus, the Roman Catholic Church, and the world:

- Saint Francis Borgia (1510–1572) established Jesuit missions in North and South America.

- Saint Peter Claver (1580–1654) aided African slaves who were shipped on slave ships to Colombia, then the world's largest slave trading port.

- Jacques Marquette (1637–1675) was a missionary and explorer who was among the first people to explore the Mississippi River.

- John Carroll (1735–1815) became the United States' first bishop and helped found Georgetown University in what would become Washington, DC.

CHAPTER THREE

BUILDING A SPIRITUAL FOUNDATION

B ergoglio's decision to join the Society of Jesus came as a surprise to his mother and father. After four years of keeping his confessional revelation secret, Bergoglio announced he was entering seminary. He had just survived a serious bout of pneumonia and was ready to embark on a new spiritual journey. While Mario was pleased with his son's decision to enter the priesthood, Regina was not. However, she eventually came to embrace the decision.

Who Are the Jesuits?

The Society of Jesus was founded in 1540 by Saint Ignatius of Loyola. Nineteen years before, Saint Ignatius had been injured and captured in a battle between the Spanish and the French in Pamplona, Spain. Ignatius's

The motto of the Jesuits is *Ad maiorem Dei gloriam*, or "For the greater glory of God." It is attributed to Saint Ignatius.

JESUITS IN ARGENTINA

Latin America was one of the first places where Jesuits established missions. The first Argentine Jesuit mission was established in the early 1600s. The mission served an indigenous community called the Guarani that had been enslaved by colonizing Spaniards. The Jesuits employed them and shared European art and culture. They also introduced them to the teachings of the Roman Catholic Church. Later, the Jesuits established schools in Buenos Aires.

Today, the ruins of Jesuit missions are popular tourist attractions. One of the most visited is San Ignacio Miní, a mission established in the Guarani community. Founded in 1611, the settlement was moved twice before it was built on its current site in 1696. Visitors can explore several well-preserved buildings, including the church, schools, and residence of the Jesuit missionaries.

courage impressed his French captors, who carried him to his home in Loyola, Spain, to recover from his injuries. During his recovery, Ignatius read religious books and prayed. After his injuries healed, Ignatius dedicated his life to God and began studying to become a priest in Paris, France. At the same time, he fasted and did charity work. In 1534, Saint Ignatius and six other men took vows and founded the Company of Jesus in Paris. In 1537, the group traveled to Italy to get permission from Pope Paul III to create a new religious order dedicated to a lifestyle of prayer, charity, and poverty. That same year, the men were ordained as priests in Venice, Italy. Three years later, on September 27, 1540, Pope Paul III signed the document that made the Society of Jesus an official order of the Roman Catholic Church.

Jesuits soon became known for their simplicity, modesty, and intelligence. The priests took vows of poverty and chastity. Another vow included specific obedience to the pope, who had the power to send Jesuits out to do missionary work. Jesuit priests practice their vows by living simply, often to the point of poverty. They do not have an official uniform but wear modest clothing that conforms to the norms of the

NOVITIATES

When men enter the Society of Jesus, they are not automatically made Jesuit priests. Like Bergoglio, they must first become a novitiate, or novice. This first stage of becoming a Jesuit is very important for both the man and the order itself.

Jesuit novitiates spend their time testing to see if the Jesuit way of life is right for them. Saint Ignatius, the founder of the Society of Jesus, designed the novitiate experience to be challenging so a novice can determine whether becoming a Jesuit priest is his true calling.

Novitiates participate in a 30-day retreat to better connect with and follow Jesus. They also undertake a trip on which they are allowed little or no money and must rely on spiritual support and the good will of others. Novitiates work in hospitals to serve the poor, dying, and mentally and physically disabled. Lastly, a novitiate lives in the Jesuit way of poverty and modesty. After successfully completing these tasks, novitiates may seek permission from Jesuit leaders to take vows. Following additional years of study, they may finally become Jesuit priests.

As a young man, Bergoglio took an intense interest in his studies.

community in which they live. Jesuits are sent across the globe on missions to spread the message of the Roman Catholic Church as well as to improve the social and economic situations in the communities where they live and work.

Early Years with the Jesuits

Two years after he joined the Society of Jesus as a novitiate, or novice, Bergoglio took his first vows as a Jesuit on March 12, 1960. He decided to join the Society of Jesus because he was impressed with the order's discipline and its focus on missionary work. His early years with the order were devoted to academic study and teaching. Bergoglio focused on obtaining a well-rounded education, a hallmark of the Jesuit order. He traveled west to Chile to study the humanities, then returned home in 1963. Back in Argentina, he studied philosophy at the Colegio de San José in the Buenos Aires suburb of San Miguel.

After he completed his studies in 1964, Bergoglio turned to teaching. However, it was not his first choice of occupation. He asked his superiors if he could travel to Japan to do missionary work, but they denied his request. They said his bout with pneumonia had weakened him, and they claimed he was not healthy enough to travel overseas. Instead, he taught high school literature and psychology for the next three years. His first assignment was at Jesuit High School in Santa Fe, Argentina. He stayed there for two years before moving onto a prestigious high school in Buenos Aires. While teaching high school, Bergoglio introduced his students to important Argentine literary figures. He was able to persuade famed Argentine writer Jorge Luis Borges to lecture for a day. Borges was one of Bergoglio's favorite writers when he was a teenager.

After finishing up his third year of teaching, Bergoglio went back to school. He returned to the Colegio de San José in San Miguel to study theology. Finally, Bergoglio was ordained as a priest on December 13, 1969. He had fulfilled his personal mission of joining the priesthood.

JORGE LUIS BORGES

Jorge Luis Borges was a poet, essayist, and short-story writer born in Buenos Aires. As a young boy, he loved books and was fluent in both English and Spanish. After spending time in Europe as a young man, Borges returned to Buenos Aires and began writing poems and short stories. He spent his adult life writing, lecturing, and working in libraries. Borges is credited with bringing Latin American literature to the world's attention. His writing is enjoyed by academics and casual readers alike.

Jesuit missionaries spread their religion across the Americas
in the centuries following the order's founding.

Bergoglio's Church

When he was ordained as a priest, Bergoglio became part of a long tradition of Roman Catholicism in Latin America. The Roman Catholic Church was one of the first European organizations to establish roots in South and Central America after Spanish explorers landed in the 1500s. In fact, Catholic missionaries were part of Christopher Columbus's team of explorers. The influence of the church can be felt in the architecture, culture, and politics of towns and cities across South America. Catholic churches can be found in most city centers and town squares. In Rio de Janeiro, Brazil, a colossal statue of Jesus watches over the city with hands outstretched.

The Roman Catholic Church has strong roots in Argentina. More than three quarters of Argentines consider themselves Roman Catholics.[2] Catholicism has a preferred status in the country's constitution even though the body of laws also protects an individual's freedom of religion. Sometimes, this relationship can create conflicts between the church and the government. Disagreements also arise between conservative and liberal Argentines. Each side uses its own interpretation of church teachings to validate its beliefs.

It was not long before Bergoglio began taking on leadership roles within the Argentine church. Only four years after his ordination, Bergoglio became a leader in the country's Jesuit order. He was well on his way to becoming one of the church's most influential figures.

CHAPTER
FOUR

TUMULTUOUS YEARS

In 1973, only four years after being ordained as a Jesuit priest, Bergoglio was chosen as father provincial of the Argentine province of the Society of Jesus. The Society of Jesus is broken up into regional organizations known as provinces. Jesuit priests called father provincials lead the provinces and serve as spiritual leaders to Jesuits in the province. During Bergoglio's tenure as father provincial, he led the province through a tumultuous time for both the Jesuits and the country of Argentina.

The Debate over Liberation Theology

Jesuits have been recognized as an official order of the Catholic Church for centuries. However, relations between the Society of Jesus and the Vatican have not always been warm. This was especially so during the

Bergoglio, *middle*, celebrates a mass in Buenos Aires in 1973.

1970s, when the Vatican denounced a new movement within the Jesuit order called liberation theology.

Liberation theology was developed in the late 1960s and became popular in the 1970s. The religious movement suggested Catholics should apply their doctrine to help the poor and those oppressed by their governments. To do so, liberation theologians argued

LIBERATION THEOLOGY: TWO VIEWPOINTS

Liberation theology's supporters believe the movement is consistent with the Bible. Former priest Phillip Berryman wrote,

> Liberation theology is an interpretation of Christian faith out of the experience of the poor. It is an attempt to read the Bible and key Christian doctrines with the eyes of the poor. . . . Liberation theology is a critique of economic structures that enable some Latin Americans to jet to Miami or London to shop, while most of their fellow citizens do not have safe drinking water.[1]

Others—especially officials within the church—argue liberation theology runs counter to Christian values. Cardinal Joseph Ratzinger, who later became Pope Benedict XVI, wrote,

> [Marxism] imposes its logic and leads the 'theologies of liberation' to accept a series of positions which are incompatible with the Christian vision of humanity. . . . In particular, the very nature of ethics is radically called into question because of the borrowing of these [ideas] from Marxism. In fact, it is the transcendent character of the distinction between good and evil, the principle of morality, which [Marxism] implicitly denie[s].[2]

Cardinal Joseph Ratzinger, who later became Pope Benedict XVI, harshly criticized liberation theology in a 1984 news conference.

they needed to become involved in the politics and civic matters of the communities in which they lived. Many believed the economic structures of Western civilization were sinful and caused social inequalities that oppressed the poor. They also believed God worked through the poor, and working with impoverished people was the only way to understand the stories in the Bible.

Because Jesuits take vows of poverty, and because missionary work among the poor is an integral part of their calling, they are perceived as being more concerned with social justice than the Roman Catholic Church as a whole. Some Latin American Jesuits in the 1960s and 1970s believed there was a fundamental difference between the Roman Catholic Church of Europe and the Roman Catholic Church of Latin America. They believed the latter should focus its efforts on serving the poor.

When some of these Jesuits began adopting the teachings of liberation theology, the leaders of the Roman Catholic Church voiced strong concerns. Pope Paul VI accused the leader of the Society of Jesus, Pedro Arrupe, of being too lenient with the Latin American Jesuit priests. He claimed Jesuits in general were of "loose discipline."[3] The Vatican continued to be critical of priests who adopted liberation theology in the 1980s. When Pope John Paul II visited Nicaragua in 1983, a priest who practiced liberation theology greeted him by kneeling before his feet. The pope wagged his finger at the man and sharply criticized him. By the 1990s, the church had curbed the influence of liberation theologians by appointing more conservative priests to leadership positions in Latin America.

As father provincial of the Jesuit province in Argentina, Bergoglio did not embrace the liberation theology movement. He claimed it was too influenced by the theories of German philosopher Karl Marx.

Marx believed that eventually, the capitalist economic system oppressing the working classes would break down and give way to a new system in which the working class would control the economy and government. This new system would evolve into a classless system Marx called Communism. However, Bergoglio did agree the poor deserved special consideration within the church and within their communities. Despite this, many believed Bergoglio was too harsh on the Jesuit priests who practiced liberation theology. Bergoglio demanded the Jesuit priests under his control avoid getting involved in the politics of the poor and instead serve them as chaplains and as parish priests. They argued Bergoglio's opposition to the movement divided the Jesuit order. The dispute surrounding liberation theology was

KARL MARX AND FRIEDRICH ENGELS

Karl Marx and Friedrich Engels were two of the most influential thinkers of the 1800s. Marx was an economist, historian, and sociologist; Engels was a German philosopher. Together, they wrote *The Communist Manifesto*, in which they promoted the idea of socialism and replacing capitalist economies with a society in which the workers form the ruling class. As father provincial, Bergoglio criticized the liberation theology movement as being too heavily influenced by the work of Karl Marx.

Army troops patrolled the streets of Buenos Aires after the 1976 coup.

not the only controversy Bergoglio faced as father provincial, however.

Argentina's Dirty War

While Catholics were battling each other over liberation theology, Argentines were subjected to a violent seven-year period known as the Dirty War (1976–1983). On March 29, 1976, the military staged a coup and deposed President Isabel Perón. In her place, the military installed a three-man junta and made Lieutenant General Jorge Rafaél Videla president of Argentina. The country was now under a violent military dictatorship. Over the next few years, a series of subsequent military dictators replaced him. Their periods of rule were as brief as a few weeks.

Soon, the junta moved to revoke Argentine citizens' civil rights. It banned trade unions, imposed censorship and curfews on Argentines, and closed the National Congress, Argentina's legislative body. The military also set up detention camps to imprison thousands of Argentines who it believed opposed its rule.

In the last few years of the Dirty War, Argentina underwent an economic decline. The economic downturn and a brief, unpopular war against the United Kingdom over the

THE FALKLAND ISLANDS

The Falkland Islands, also called the Malvinas Islands, are a group of two big islands and hundreds of smaller ones off the southeast coast of Argentina. Though the Falkland Islands are self-governing, the islands are considered territories of the United Kingdom. This claim has created conflict between the United Kingdom and Argentina since the 1800s. On April 2, 1982, Argentine president Leopoldo Galtieri started a ten-week war against the United Kingdom over the islands. After hundreds of deaths on each side, Argentine troops surrendered to British troops in the Falkland Islands' largest town, Stanley. Both the United Kingdom and Argentina still claim ownership over the islands.

Falkland Islands may have turned more Argentines against the military dictatorship. By 1982, President Reynaldo Bignone began allowing Argentines to vote in general elections and organize political parties. However, by the time the Dirty War ended in 1983, 10,000 to 30,000 Argentine civilians had been killed by the military dictatorship government, including many who were kidnapped and never heard from again.[4] These people became known as the *desaparecidos*, or "disappeared ones."

In 1983, Argentines elected a new president, Raúl Alfonsín. Alfonsín was not part of the military. Instead, he was a member of a center-left political party called the Radical Civic Union. His administration put some of the military government leaders on trial, including former dictators. However, the National Congress later passed laws giving immunity to hundreds of low-ranking military personnel. That meant these individuals could not be tried for crimes they may have committed during the Dirty War.

The Church's Role in the Dirty War

The Roman Catholic Church was caught in the middle of the Dirty War. Throughout the military dictatorship, the church failed to openly oppose the government's violation of the civil rights of Argentinians. However, individual church leaders either openly criticized or supported the dictatorship. Some of these leaders—including Bergoglio—became the subject of anger and criticism after the Dirty War was over.

Bergoglio served as father provincial during the first three years of the Dirty War. In May 1976, military personnel kidnapped two Jesuit priests whom they accused of speaking out against the dictatorship. The priests were released after being tortured. Years later, an investigation by Argentine journalist Horacio Verbitsky claimed Bergoglio turned the priests over to the military. Bergoglio has emphatically denied this claim. Shortly after

HORACIO VERBITSKY

Since 1960, Argentine investigative journalist Horacio Verbitsky has dedicated his career to battling press censorship and exposing corruption in the government. His determination to uncover the truth has earned him the nickname *el perro*, or "the dog." Argentina's Dirty War has become a familiar topic for Verbitsky. Before writing *The Silence*, in which he makes claims about Bergoglio's involvement in the kidnapping of two Jesuit priests, Verbitsky published *The Flight*. The book contains the confessions of a military official in the military dictatorship government. It details the kidnapping, torture, and killing of Argentines during the Dirty War.

A memorial wall lists the names of people
killed during Argentina's Dirty War.

Bergoglio was elected pope in 2013, one of the priests who had been kidnapped affirmed Bergoglio had not directly handed the priests to the government. The priest did not know if Bergoglio was indirectly involved in the kidnapping.

After the Dirty War, people also criticized Bergoglio for failing to lead the Jesuit order strongly against the military dictatorship. They claimed Bergoglio and the church knew about the government's kidnappings and other civil rights violations but did nothing to protest the government's actions. Instead, critics claimed, the church openly endorsed the dictatorship. However, supporters of Bergoglio argued failing to challenge the dictatorship was a practical move on the father provincial's part. They also believed Bergoglio has not fully disclosed his role in opposing the military coup due to humility. In 2010, Bergoglio claimed to have hid people in his church during the Dirty War and helped people escape the junta. The debate over the church and Bergoglio's role in the Dirty War was renewed once Bergoglio was elected pope.

CHAPTER
FIVE

LOWLY BUT CHOSEN

Bergoglio ended his tenure as father provincial of the Argentine province of the Society of Jesus in the midst of the Dirty War. However, he continued to work within the church to help rebuild its influence on Argentine society. This work did not go unnoticed. Eventually, Bergoglio became one of the most influential Latin Americans in the Roman Catholic Church.

A Return to Teaching and Learning

In 1980, after he left his post as father provincial, Bergoglio took a teaching position at the Colegio de San José, where he had studied as a young man. It was very rare for such a high-ranking priest to take a teaching position. In addition to his position at the Colegio de San José, Bergoglio also became a parish priest for the town of San Miguel.

Bergoglio climbed the ranks of the Roman Catholic Church in the 1980s and 1990s.

After serving for six years in San Miguel, Bergoglio traveled to Germany to finish his doctoral degree. His superiors in the church then sent him back to Buenos Aires to teach at the Colegio del Salvador, a college at which he had previously taught. Church officials then moved Bergoglio to Córdoba, a city in the north-central region of Argentina. There, he served as the spiritual director of a local Jesuit church. He stayed for a few years until he received a new appointment in 1992.

Leading Argentina's Catholics

On May 20, 1992, Bergoglio received notice he had been chosen as a bishop of Buenos Aires. The appointment came from the leader of the Roman Catholic Church, Pope John Paul II. Pope John Paul II appointed Bergoglio as the auxiliary bishop of Buenos Aires at the request of Cardinal Antonio Quarracino, who was serving as the archbishop of Buenos Aires. An auxiliary bishop assists a bishop whose diocese is too large for one person to oversee. Cardinal Quarracino wanted to work with Bergoglio more closely. A week later, Bergoglio took office and chose the motto and coat of arms that would represent him as bishop. His motto, *miserando atque eligendo*, or "lowly but chosen," reflected his commitment to the Jesuit way of poverty and modesty. His coat of arms included the symbol of the Society of Jesus: the initials *IHS*.

As auxiliary bishop, Bergoglio kept a low profile and spent his time in the community. His duties included counseling priests, hearing confessions, preaching, and overseeing the Catholic university in Buenos Aires. During his tenure as auxiliary bishop of Buenos Aires, he was also appointed the episcopal vicar of the Flores district where he grew up.

COATS OF ARMS

Coats of arms have been used by nobility for hundreds of years. They were used to identify troops in battle and were passed down through families. Popes have had their own coats of arms for at least 800 years to mark buildings, decrees, publications, and other documents. Papal coats of arms can be original designs, a family shield, or the coats of arms the pope used as a bishop. When he became pope, Bergoglio chose to continue using his bishop coat of arms.

The symbols on Bergoglio's coat of arms carried over to the coat of arms he would later use as Pope Francis.

Episcopal vicars are bishops appointed to oversee part of a diocese.

On December 21, 1993, Bergoglio was appointed the vicar general of the Archdiocese of Buenos Aires. This post is the second highest in an archdiocese. The vicar general acts as the archbishop's second in command, performing administrative duties and overseeing the clergy in the diocese's area. When Bergoglio was appointed as vicar general, he was on his way toward becoming the archbishop of Buenos Aires.

In early 1998, a little more than four years after Bergoglio was appointed vicar general, Archbishop Quarracino passed away. Bergoglio became the front-runner to succeed Quarracino. On February 28, 1998, Pope John Paul II named Bergoglio as the archbishop of Buenos Aires. Three years later, in 2001, Pope John Paul II made Bergoglio a cardinal. Bergoglio would now

HIERARCHY IN THE ROMAN CATHOLIC CHURCH

The Roman Catholic Church is a highly structured organization with multiple levels of hierarchy. The smallest organization is the Catholic parish. The parish is the local level of the church and is led by a priest. There are more than 400,000 Catholic priests worldwide. The parish is the level at which most Catholics interact with the church. Parishes are part of a broader organization called a diocese. A diocese is run by a bishop. The next largest organization is the archdiocese, which is led by an archbishop. Sometimes, archbishops are also cardinals and have responsibilities at the Catholic Church's headquarters in Vatican City.

The United States contains an important and sizable part of the Roman Catholic Church's hierarchy. There are 19 cardinals in the United States, along with 440 bishops. They serve 145 dioceses and 33 archdioceses.[2] More than 2,000 dioceses exist worldwide. The pope lives in the Vatican, where he governs all of these dioceses. Together, they make up the entirety of the Roman Catholic Church.

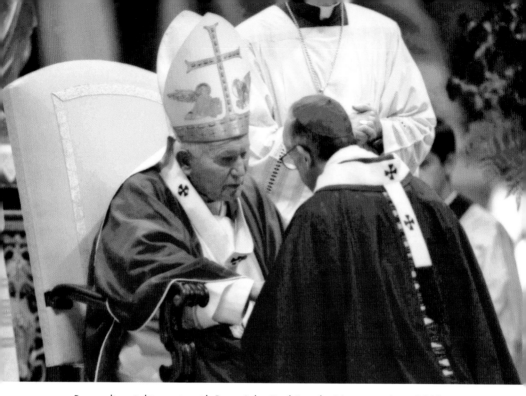

Bergoglio, *right*, meets with Pope John Paul II at the Vatican in June 1998.

have responsibilities at the Vatican in Rome as well as in Buenos Aires.

As archbishop and cardinal, Bergoglio continued to live by the vows of the Society of Jesus, which required him to live in modesty and poverty. Other archbishops lived in mansions provided by the church. Bergoglio turned down this housing and instead rented a room next to the Metropolitan Cathedral, Buenos Aires's largest Catholic church. In keeping with his Jesuit vows, Bergoglio's room contained only a bed, a small stove, a desk, a chair, and a radio so he could listen to soccer games. Instead of a private car, he used public transportation to get around the city.

As archbishop, Bergoglio focused his efforts on four goals. He worked to create more open and brotherly communities, assist the poor and the sick, and support the clergy and lay members of his diocese. He created new parishes throughout Argentina and reorganized some of the offices within the archdiocese. All of these goals worked toward rebuilding the church's influence on Argentina's culture and society.

A major part of rebuilding the church's influence was reintroducing traditional Catholic values back into society. When Bergoglio became archbishop, Argentina's economy was close to collapse. Bergoglio blamed unregulated capitalism for the downturn that left many Argentines

BUENOS AIRES'S METROPOLITAN CATHEDRAL

When he became an archbishop and then a cardinal, Bergoglio's home church became the magnificent Metropolitan Cathedral in Buenos Aires's main square, the Plaza de Mayo. The cathedral has gone through six different buildings since its construction in 1593. The current building was completed in 1911. It is an example of neoclassical architecture and has 12 Greek columns that represent Jesus's 12 apostles. The Metropolitan Cathedral holds the tombs of several military generals as well as Argentina's Tomb of the Unknown Soldier.

impoverished and condemned the "demonic effects of the imperialism of money."[3] Many Argentines agreed with Bergoglio.

Bergoglio also resisted many social changes, including the legalization of same-sex marriage, adoption by same-sex couples, and access to free contraception. His stance against these reforms drew criticism from Argentina's president Cristina Fernández de Kirchner, who was elected in 2007. She claimed Bergoglio's opposition to these social changes would "send us back to medieval times."[4] These same stances would later attract attention and criticism when Bergoglio became Pope Francis. However, he gave Kirchner a warm reception when they met in the Vatican shortly after his election.

Apologizing for the Dirty War

In 2012, Cardinal Bergoglio decided to address the church's controversial behavior during the Dirty War of the 1970s. In October 2012, the bishops of Argentina, led by Bergoglio, issued a formal apology to the people of Argentina for the church's inability to protect Argentines from the oppression by the military dictatorship. However, many Argentines were not satisfied with the apology. Detractors said it did little to help ongoing investigations of human rights violations.

Cardinal Bergoglio also condemned the Argentine dictatorships of the 1970s and 1980s in a 2012 address. He claimed during the Dirty War, Argentina was a victim of corruption, dictatorships, cults of personality, and the pursuit of power by a few individuals. His words resonated with Argentines who had grown tired of political personalities. Despite this move, however, Bergoglio has been reluctant to publicly speak about his role in the Dirty War. He has twice refused to testify in court about human rights violations of which he was allegedly aware. Church leaders in Argentina have the right to refuse to testify in court. Though he volunteered to testify in 2010, his critics believed his answers did not address the question completely.

> "We share everyone's pain and once again ask the forgiveness of everyone we failed or didn't support as we should have."[5]
> —The bishops of Argentina in 2012 on the church's actions during the military dictatorship and Dirty War

Working in Vatican City

Since Bergoglio was both an archbishop and a cardinal, his responsibilities included work in Vatican City as

Bergoglio walks to a Vatican meeting a few
weeks before becoming Pope Francis.

well as in Argentina. As a cardinal, Bergoglio served on
several committees that helped oversee the government
and spiritual direction of the Roman Catholic Church.

In Rome, Bergoglio was a member of the
Congregation of Divine Worship and Sacraments and
the Congregation of Institutes of Consecrated Life. The
first group oversees how church services and ceremonies
are conducted. The second group is responsible for
regulating the government, discipline, studies, and
rights of religious orders and similar societies. Bergoglio

was also a member of the Congregation of Clergy, which maintains the quality of the clergy around the world. It also oversees the various hierarchical organizations to which the clergy belong.

Another responsibility Bergoglio undertook in his work at the Vatican is to sit on the Pontifical Council for the Family and the Pontifical Commission for Latin America. The Pontifical Council for the Family supports the efforts of the church in helping build stronger Christian families and coordinates the church's family-related efforts, especially those surrounding the issues of contraception, abortion, sex education, and marriage. As a member of the council, Cardinal Bergoglio emphasized the "immeasurable richness of the vocation to a life of matrimony and family as a foundation of society and the Church."[6] The Pontifical Commission for Latin America coordinates the church's efforts to promote Roman Catholicism in Latin America. It also supports the clergy serving in Latin American countries.

Participation in this diverse group of committees helped Bergoglio understand the complex needs and objectives of the church. It prepared him for what would become his most challenging post yet.

CHAPTER
SIX

TINY NATION, LARGEST RELIGION

A cross the Tiber River from the center of Rome, Italy, sits the world's smallest independent nation-state, Vatican City. Surrounded by the city of Rome on all sides, Vatican City is the headquarters of the Roman Catholic Church and Pope Francis's home. The church has occupied this land since the 300s.

In approximately 324 CE, Constantine I, the emperor of the Roman Empire, began construction on a church near the marshy bank of the Tiber River of Rome. Constantine I was the first Roman emperor to convert to Christianity. He spent his reign turning the empire into a Christian state. Christianity was recognized as a religion in Constantine's Edict of Milan shortly before he began construction on the Vatican.

Over the next 1,700 years, the Catholic Church raised walls and constructed buildings at the Vatican. There are six entrances to the city, but only three

Vatican City occupies only approximately 110 acres (44 ha).

are open to the public. The largest building is Saint Peter's Basilica, where Pope Francis was announced as the new pope on March 13, 2013. Adjacent to Saint Peter's Basilica on its east side is Saint Peter's Square. The square was built in the 1600s by Italian architect and sculptor Gian Lorenzo Bernini. Bernini's keyhole-shaped design focuses visitors' attention on the facade of Saint Peter's Basilica. Saint Peter's Square is where Catholics around the world come to watch the pope give his Christmas and Easter blessings and to welcome a new pope.

Another important building inside the Vatican is the Apostolic Palace, the building in which most recent popes have lived. Pope Nicholas V started construction on the pope's residence in the 1400s, but each new pope continued to decorate and remodel it through the 1500s. Today, the third floor of the Apostolic Palace is reserved for the pope's private residence. Seven large rooms, including a bedroom, a study, and a chapel, make up the papal apartments. Other parts of the palace are used by Vatican employees. Pope Francis has decided to forgo this lavish residence to live in a small guest house on the grounds of Vatican City.

People of Vatican City

The pope is not the only one who lives in Vatican City, however. The Vatican is also home to hundreds of employees who handle the day-to-day operations of the world's smallest independent nation-state. Most of the Vatican's non-clergy workers live in Rome and are citizens of Italy. Within the Vatican's medieval walls is a city with its own government, security, media, and post office. These institutions and the

BERNINI'S INTENT FOR SAINT PETER'S SQUARE

Gian Lorenzo Bernini was a favorite artist of Catholic leaders in the 1600s, including cardinals and popes. He helped shape the Baroque style of art, which is distinctive for its richness, grandeur, ornateness, and drama. Bernini wanted Saint Peter's Square to reflect the Catholic Church's growing influence on the world:

> Considering that Saint Peter's is almost the matrix of all the churches, its portico had to give an open-armed, maternal welcome to all Catholics, confirming their faith; to heretics, reconciling them with the Church; and to the infidels, enlightening them about the true faith.[1]

Pope Francis has avoided many of the luxurious aspects of being pope, including the use of the Apostolic Palace.

people who manage them are responsible for keeping the Vatican up and running.

Though it must import its food, water, electricity, and gas from Rome, Vatican City is considered a self-sufficient state. It has its own system of government called the Holy See. Though the pope is the head of state of Vatican City, the president of the Pontifical Commission oversees government duties. The Holy See governs the Vatican's bank, pharmacy, post office, telephone system, and television and radio stations.

In addition to Pope Francis, people who call the Vatican home include cardinals, scholars, librarians, seminary students, and restoration specialists who take care of the Vatican's many antiquities. Some of the more colorful residents of the Vatican are the members of the Swiss Guard, an organization that has protected the pope since 1506. The Vatican is supported by the donations of Catholics around the world, and its residents are not subject to income tax. The Vatican's employees help maintain and support one of the world's oldest religions.

A Brief History of the Roman Catholic Church

The Roman Catholic Church claims to have maintained historical continuity dating back to Peter and the

SWISS GUARDS

For more than 500 years, Swiss Guards have stood watch over Vatican City. In 1506, a group of mercenaries from Switzerland arrived at the Vatican at the request of Pope Julius II. Pope Julius II, sometimes known as the Warrior Pope, was afraid the warring Italian territories surrounding the Vatican would strike at the city. His fears were not unfounded. Just a dozen years before, French monarch King Charles VIII had invaded the Vatican and the surrounding lands owned by the church.

Since Pope Julius II hired them in 1506, the Swiss Guards have been responsible for the security of Vatican City. All guardsmen are young, unmarried Swiss men who must be Catholics. They are only considered for the post upon the recommendation of their parish priest and must have completed military school in Switzerland. Swiss Guardsmen wear traditional uniforms with broad yellow, blue, and red stripes, black berets, and belts with buckles inscribed with the monogram of the Pontifical Guard.

SAINT PETER

The Roman Catholic Church recognizes Saint Peter as the first in an unbroken line of popes and as the leader of the early church after Jesus's crucifixion. Peter's original name was Simon, but Jesus gave him a new name, Peter, which comes from the Latin word *petra*, or "rock." Though much about Peter's life and work is unknown, church tradition, supported by some religious documents, claims Peter was martyred in Rome during the reign of the Roman Emperor Nero. The church did not create a system for formal canonization, or creation of saints, until the 1200s, so the early church simply declared Peter a saint after his death. Today, Catholics celebrate Saint Peter in five festivals throughout the year.[2]

apostles of Jesus. This would make Catholicism the oldest Christian religion in the world. In fact, until the Reformation in the 1300s to 1500s, the Roman Catholic Church was known simply as Christianity. According to church doctrine, Peter was one of Jesus's most outspoken followers. He was a leader among Jesus's disciples and continued to lead the new church after Jesus's crucifixion. Theologians and historians have a difficult time verifying Peter's residence, death, and burial in Rome. Still, the Roman Catholic Church credits Peter with bringing the church to the city.

In approximately 330 CE, just a few years after he ordered the beginning of construction on Saint Peter's Basilica, Constantine I moved the government of the Roman Empire from Rome to Constantinople, now

Artists often depict Peter holding keys, symbolizing the keys to heaven.

Istanbul, in Turkey. With the government out of the way, the move gave the pope the opportunity to increase the church's influence in Rome and the surrounding area. Because of this, the pope decided not to move the church's headquarters to Constantinople.

After the fall of the Roman Empire in 476, Christians throughout the empire migrated to Europe, bringing their religion with them. Through the rest of the Middle Ages, the power of the pope grew, church missionaries traveled farther and farther to spread the teachings of the church, and church leaders helped solidify church traditions and institutions. Not all these changes came peacefully. Between the 1000s and the 1200s, the church funded wars in the Middle East to stop the spread of Islam, recapture formerly Christian lands, and regain control of the Holy Land. These battles have become known collectively as the Crusades. However, the church also established Christian schools and universities, and education became a powerful way to increase the church's influence in the communities it served.

By the 1300s, some Christians became increasingly unhappy with some of the practices of

THE CRUSADES

A crusade is a war conducted in the name of religion. Between the 1000s and 1200s, the Catholic Church waged Crusades against the spread of Islam, against pagans, and to reconquer previously Christian lands. Though crusaders saw the battles as a spiritual struggle for redemption from sin, the Crusades are now considered a dark chapter in the history of the church.

the church and began to seek an alternative to the established Christian church. As a result, over the next 200 years, the church experienced a period of unrest that culminated in a period called the Reformation that started in the early 1500s. Some Christians were weary of corruption and greed within the church as well as the church's practice of selling indulgences. Indulgences were pardons from sin that the church granted to churchgoers. At first, indulgences were granted after the recipient served in the Crusades or committed good works such as charity or pilgrimages. Over time, however, indulgences were increasingly granted to those who made monetary contributions to the church. In 1517, a young friar named Martin Luther published a scathing critique of the church's system of indulgences, one of the first steps in a process known as the Reformation.

During the Reformation, many Christians broke off from the church to form a new Christian tradition, Protestantism. At this point, the Christian Church was redefined as the Roman Catholic Church. Though the decades of the Reformation were tumultuous for the Roman Catholic Church, when they were over, the church had reformed some internal issues that had been plaguing it, strengthening the Roman Catholic Church as an organization.

From the late 1400s throughout the 1500s, explorers from Spain and other countries explored and conquered much of South and Central America. Among the explorers were missionaries from the Roman Catholic Church who were sent to convert native peoples. Later, missionaries from the Society of Jesus also traveled to Latin America. When Bergoglio entered the Society of Jesus in 1958, he was joining a long tradition of Jesuits in Latin America.

Over the next few centuries, the church faced new challenges from outside forces. In the 1600s and 1700s, a new intellectual movement in Europe called the Enlightenment changed scholars' worldviews. During this period, scholars employed logic, reason, and science, rather than religious faith, to understand the world around them. They then sought to use this knowledge to improve their lives. Thinkers during the Enlightenment believed embracing reason would bring individuals freedom and happiness. These ideas were then applied to religion, threatening to undermine the influence and role of the Roman Catholic Church on people's lives and views of the world.

In the latter half of the 1700s, upheaval in France also threatened the church. To many who wished to change France's political structure from a monarchy to a democracy, the Catholic Church was an ally of the king. When the French lower classes took action during the French Revolution (1787–1799), they targeted the church as well as the ruling classes. The entire church structure in France was reorganized, and the pope was stripped of all authority except over spiritual matters. In 1798, French troops marched on the Vatican in Rome, forcing the leader of the Roman Catholic Church, Pope Pius VI, to flee the city. The next year, Pope Pius VI was captured. He later died in France. There were whispers of getting rid of the role of pope. The church's influence and power were quickly declining.

Fortunately for the church, Napoléon I came to power in 1799. Though he was a revolutionary,

Relationships between the church and governments are still important. Pope Francis met with United Nations General Assembly president Vuk Jeremić in 2013.

Napoléon I believed the French people needed organized religion. He was able to negotiate between France and the church and institute several reforms to the Catholic Church in France. The reforms were outlined in the Concordat of 1801, an agreement between Napoléon I and Pope Pius VII. It gave freedom of worship to French citizens, acknowledging most French people were practicing Catholics. The Concordat of 1801, along with later reforms, helped create Vatican City as a sovereign state under the control of the pope by the late 1800s.

While the Concordat of 1801 helped restore some of the church's influence in Europe, it became a source of conflict between Napoléon I and the church. When Pope Pius VII refused to adopt amendments reducing the pope's authority in France, he was arrested and put in prison. But Pope Pius VII outlived Napoléon I, and soon he was able to reestablish his authority over all church matters. He took steps to create relationships with the governments of newly established countries in Latin America, strengthen religious orders such as the Society of Jesus, and expand the church's influence on art and education. The church was once again a powerful institution going into the 1900s. Its new relationships with Latin American countries made it possible for cardinals to elect the first Latin American pope, Pope Francis, more than 200 years later.

CHAPTER
SEVEN

A SPIRITUAL PHILOSOPHY

When Bergoglio entered the priesthood in the 1960s, he joined a religion with a rich history and long-established doctrine and traditions. These elements helped shape Bergoglio's philosophy and theology. While some of his beliefs reflect the socially conservative nature of the Catholic Church, others reflect the high value the Jesuits place on social justice. When Bergoglio became Pope Francis in March 2013, he brought his philosophy with him, and the world expects these values will guide his decisions as leader of the Roman Catholic Church.

Pope Francis on Modern Issues

Pope Francis's stance on modern issues reflects the traditional social doctrine of the Roman Catholic Church. He is a critic of what he calls "the imperialism of money" and globalization of world economies.[1]

Pope Francis introduced his unique mix of traditional beliefs and social justice to the highest level of the Roman Catholic Church.

As such, he is also an opponent of the policies of the International Monetary Fund, whose mission is to help build financial stability and cooperation between nations.

Pope Francis has also been a staunch critic of a departure from traditional values since his opposition to progressive liberation theology in the 1970s. His position has invited conflict from Argentine presidents whose social policies have been increasingly socially progressive. In 2010, then-cardinal Bergoglio led a march and made a speech against the president's proposed bill to legalize same-sex marriage in Argentina, explaining that "the essence of being a human [is] the union of a man and a woman . . . as the natural path for procreation."[2] President Cristina Fernández de Kirchner heavily criticized Bergoglio's stance. In addition to opposing same-sex marriage, Pope Francis also believes

Pope Francis met with President Kirchner shortly after his election in March 2013.

adoption of a child by a same-sex couple goes against the doctrine of the church.

Pope Francis holds similarly conservative views on sexual health issues. He again butted heads with President Kirchner over her plan to provide free contraception and artificial insemination to Argentines. Following church doctrine, Pope Francis also opposed the Argentine Supreme Court's 2006 decision to allow victims of rape the option of a legal abortion.

Understanding Pope Francis's Inner Jesuit

Despite his conservative views on social issues, Pope Francis strongly supports giving aid to the poor and spreading religious beliefs to them, the hallmarks of the Jesuit order to which he belongs. Jesuits are considered by some in the church to be more liberal and concerned with social justice than other Roman Catholic organizations or the church in general. Shortly after being elected pope, Pope Francis declared he "would like a poor church . . . for the poor."[3]

In the month following Pope Francis's election, it became clear he would continue to live simply, as he did as archbishop in Argentina. There, he regularly cooked his own meals, took public transportation, and visited the poor. He declined many requests for interviews over the years, choosing to stay out of the public eye, even when his critics were outspoken against him. Though he lived humbly, Pope Francis continued to enjoy tango music and soccer, as he did when he was a young man.

As pope, instead of adopting the lavish dress other popes embraced, such as ornate robes, Pope Francis wears a plain, white cassock. Following his two predecessors, John Paul II and Benedict XVI, Francis avoided using the papal throne used until 1978 to carry popes through Saint Peter's square on the shoulders of attendants. After giving his first blessing as pope, he chose to travel back to the Vatican hotel the Casa Santa Marta, where he and his fellow cardinals were staying for conclave, in a bus rather than in a private car. During conclave and other Vatican meetings as a cardinal, Pope Francis always tried to find a seat in the back of the room, choosing to keep a low profile instead of pursuing notoriety. As pope, he has declined living in the papal apartments in the lavish Apostolic Palace. Instead, he resides in room 201 in the Casa Santa Marta, which has a large living room area so Pope Francis can host guests. Pope Francis is expected to maintain his humble lifestyle and lead the church by his example. Some believe he may return the concept of a humble, soft-spoken leader back to the Roman Catholic Church.

What's in a Name?

When Cardinal Bergoglio was elected pope, he got to choose a new papal name. He picked one no other pope had ever selected: Francis. The name honors the life and legacy of Saint Francis of Assisi. Saint Francis was born the son of a merchant in approximately 1181 CE. As an adult, he turned away from his comfortable life to live in poverty. Saint Francis was intensely interested in how

THE CASA SANTA MARTA

The Casa Santa Marta is a guesthouse within the Vatican that accommodates cardinals and other visitors on official business with the pope as well as dozens of bishops and priests who work in Vatican City. Though the Casa Santa Marta is a relatively new building by Vatican standards, it was constructed on the site of an old hospice that served the poor. The hospice was built in 1891 to serve impoverished Romans. Later, it became the headquarters of the Vatican's pharmacy, and during World War II (1939–1945) the hospice hosted refugees and diplomats when Rome was under German and then Allied occupation. In 1996, Pope John Paul II ordered the old hospice be torn down to make way for the construction of a place where cardinals could live during papal conclaves. This new building became known as the Casa Santa Marta.

Saint Francis is remembered for his twin devotions to nature and poverty.

THE WOLF OF GUBBIO

Saint Francis is the patron saint of animals and ecology, as well as the patron saint of Italy. These distinctions reflect the Italian's love and respect for nature and animals, even if these animals seem threatening. Legend has it that Saint Francis helped save the town of Gubbio, Italy, from an aggressive wolf. According to the story, Saint Francis sat down with the wolf and noticed that it had a thorn in its paw. Saint Francis removed the thorn and made a deal with the wolf. If the wolf promised to not harm the town, the town would feed the wolf.

Jesus lived his life and wanted his own life to reflect Jesus's as closely as possible. Saint Francis was so devoted to his way of living he considered poverty his "lady" or "wife."

Saint Francis also had great respect for nature, including the plants and animals that surrounded him throughout his life. He was known to preach sermons to animals and would refer to the sun as "Brother Sun," the moon as "Sister Moon," and to death as "Sister Death." Later in his life, he created the Franciscan order of monks and the women's Order of Saint Clare so others who wished to live like him could do so. Saint Francis and the individuals who entered his orders took vows of poverty and charity. Charismatic and full of enthusiasm for the church and its teachings, Saint Francis was a popular figure in his time and remains so today. Pope Francis's decision to take his name shows the pope's commitment to living simply and among the poor, as Saint Francis did.

Pope Francis's spiritual philosophy and experience leading the Latin American Catholic Church should serve him well as pope. He will need a solid strength of conviction to tackle several controversial issues confronting the church today.

CHAPTER
EIGHT

LOOKING TOWARD THE FUTURE

The day after he was elected, Pope Francis gave his first mass as pope. His remarks were brief and delivered in Italian, rather than Latin as his predecessor, Pope Emeritus Benedict XVI, preferred. During the mass, he asked cardinals to find the courage to move the church forward using Catholic spiritual values rather than secular ones. "When we don't walk, we are stuck," he explained. "When we don't build on the rock, what happens? It's what happens to children when they build a sand castle and it all then falls down."[1]

The message to the cardinals and all Catholics was clear. To move forward, the church had to work within the teachings, doctrine, and traditions of Roman Catholicism. There was much work to be done. In recent years, the church had been mired in a sex abuse scandal, an internal administrative scandal referred to in the press as "VatiLeaks," and mounting challenges from

Soon after his election, Pope Francis began to navigate the challenges that faced the Roman Catholic Church.

WHAT IS A POPE EMERITUS?

When Pope Benedict XVI resigned in February 2013, he became the first pope in nearly 600 years to do so.[2] Since a pope's resignation is such a rare event, the Vatican had to come up with a system to handle Pope Benedict XVI's retirement. Most popes' tenures end at death, so there has not been a need for a title for a resigned or retired pope. The Vatican decided Benedict XVI would keep his papal name rather than revert back to his given name Joseph Ratzinger, but instead of the title "pope," he would be given the title "pope emeritus," which roughly means "retired pope." Pope Emeritus Benedict XVI now lives in the Vatican in a nunnery renovated to suit the needs of a retired life of prayer.

liberals over the church's stance on social issues such as same-sex marriage and abortion.

Sex Abuse Scandal

During the later years of Pope John Paul II's tenure, allegations of sexual abuse against children perpetrated by Catholic priests began to surface. In 2001 in Boston, Massachusetts, Archbishop Cardinal Bernard F. Law filed a court document admitting he had promoted priest John J. Geoghan even though he know Geoghan had abused seven boys.

The admission sparked an enormous investigation of sex abuse in the Boston diocese. In the process, it was revealed dozens of priests had abused children, the diocese and Cardinal Law knew about the abuse, and instead of defrocking the priests, they had moved them from

Cardinal Law left the United States after his resignation. He moved to the Vatican, where he still holds a high position in the church.

parish to parish. Catholics within the Boston area were outraged. They protested outside area churches and withheld donations to the church. Soon, victims from around the globe came forward to accuse priests of abusing them as children. Priests in the Boston area soon faced criminal charges, and the diocese was faced with several multimillion dollar lawsuits. In December 2002, Cardinal Law traveled to the Vatican to discuss the allegations with Pope John Paul II. On December 13, the pope accepted Cardinal Law's resignation.

Over the next decade, allegations of sexual abuse continued to surface around the world. During Pope Benedict XVI's eight years as pope, thousands more victims accused priests of abuse and bishops and other church leaders of covering up the crimes.[3] The church estimates approximately 1.5 to 5 percent of clergy were involved in the abuse.[4] As a cardinal, Pope Benedict XVI had dealt with sex abuse cases in his own diocese in Germany. As pope, Benedict apologized to the victims and met with them in person. He also changed the church's policies regarding youth and provided information about the scandal on the Vatican's Web site. When he heard a popular seminary priest was abusing students, Pope Benedict XVI banished him. However, he was never able to reform the church in a way that put a stop to the abuse, and he did not defrock the priests who committed the crimes.

Between 2004 and 2011, the church paid out more than $2 billion in lawsuit settlements.[6]

Going forward, Pope Francis will need to find a way to move the church beyond the sex abuse scandal. Doing so will require many changes within the church, including finding a way to better protect children, developing a system that ensures guilty priests are punished, and taking other actions that will restore Catholics' faith in the church. Some dioceses have already taken steps to prevent abuse, increase reporting, and handle past cases of abuse. Perhaps Pope Francis will use some of these systems to roll out reforms on a global scale.

VatiLeaks: Scandal Inside the Vatican

The sex abuse scandal was not the only controversy facing the Roman Catholic Church when Pope Francis was elected. In 2011, a collection of Vatican letters was published that triggered a scandal inside the Roman Curia, the administrative body of the Holy See. The letters exposed corruption within the government, including instances of bribery. One letter noted how an executive of the auto company Mercedes-Benz asked to meet with Pope Benedict XVI to suggest improvements to the Popemobile, while another described how an Italian industrialist tried to gain favor with the pope by giving him $100,000 worth of truffles.[7] In addition, the letters uncovered many instances of cardinals and other church leaders asking for personal favors from the pope.

The VatiLeaks scandal uncovered how bureaucratic the structure of the Vatican has become over the centuries. The government resembles a monarchy, where the pope is as revered as a king and the church leaders immediately below him compete for the pope's favor. This system makes church leaders susceptible to bribes and other corruption in pursuit of becoming closer to the pope. Since the pope focuses his efforts on spiritually leading the church, many of

THE POPEMOBILE

Popes have been riding in cars for nearly 100 years. Pope Pius XI, who served between 1922 and 1939, was the first pope to use a car to get around. While the pope is able to use his own vehicle when traveling in and around the Vatican, he is not able to take his car with him overseas. Instead, cars are prepared in the countries the pope plans to visit and then approved by the Vatican.

The pope's vehicle got the nickname Popemobile in 1979 after Pope John Paul II's visit to Ireland. In 1981, there was an assassination attempt on Pope John Paul II while he was in the Popemobile, prompting the addition of a bulletproof glass box placed over the area where the pope rides. Popes have the option of lowering the glass to eliminate the barrier between them and their followers.

Vatican butler Paolo Gabriele, *left*, was sentenced to prison for leaking documents. Pope Benedict XVI later pardoned him.

the administrative duties fall on the shoulders of the secretary of state, a cardinal who acts as the gatekeeper between the pope and the rest of the Roman Curia. This structure contributes to the competition among cardinals and other Vatican leaders. Additionally, since most church leaders are never punished for their corruption, they are not held accountable for their actions.

Many popes before Pope Francis have tried to reform the Vatican's system of bureaucracy but have failed because the structure of the government is so complex. "Whoever is appointed [pope], they get absorbed by the structure. Instead of you transforming the structure, the structure transforms you," explains a former leader of a Catholic order.[8] When Pope Francis was installed, Pope Emeritus Benedict XVI gave him a report on the leaks. Pope Emeritus Benedict XVI had kept the report from prying eyes in the Vatican and the press, claiming he wanted Pope Francis to have the first look at the report and decide whether or not to make the information public. Whatever Pope Francis chooses to do with the report, the problem of corruption within the Roman Curia is one controversy he will need to address during his tenure as pope.

Church Policy on Modern Issues

As the leader of the Roman Catholic Church, Pope Francis must also help the church take a stance on several hot-button issues facing Catholics, the church, and society as a whole. One of these controversial topics is same-sex marriage. While the church is officially opposed to same-sex marriage, many Catholics around the world support it and would like the Roman Catholic Church to evolve its stance on the issue. A 2013 poll of Catholics in the United States, for example, found 60 percent of respondents support same-sex marriage.[9]

Other social issues the church will continue to tackle are contraceptives and abortion. Some Catholics would like the church to modernize its stance against the use of contraceptives. Many Catholics support the church's opposition to abortion in its interest in preserving life, though some of these Catholics do not oppose abortion in all circumstances as the church does.

Other controversial topics the church faces are internal. In the United States, a group of nuns are under scrutiny by the Vatican for advocating what some Vatican officials call "radical feminist themes incompatible with the Catholic faith."[10] Though the Vatican has praised the humanitarian work the nuns have done in the United States, it has accused them of failing to work within the teachings of the church. The sisters are now overseen by two bishops and one archbishop,

A POLL OF US CATHOLICS

In early 2013, the *New York Times* and CBS News took a poll of nearly 1,600 Roman Catholics in the United States. They found many US Catholics would like the church to update its views on several controversial topics. Seventy percent of people who responded to the poll wanted the church to allow Catholics to use contraception, priests to marry, and women to become priests. Nearly two-thirds of respondents favored legalizing same-sex marriage.[11] Most Catholics in the survey believed their parish priests understood the modern needs of Catholics.

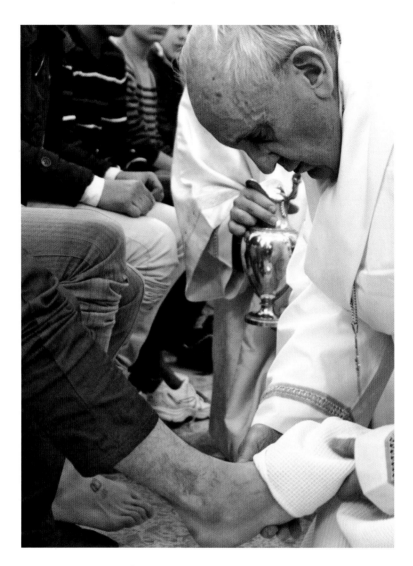

In March 2013, Pope Francis demonstrated his commitment
to society's weakest members by washing the feet of
inmates at a juvenile detention center in Rome.

who are revising the sisters' programs and the speakers
they sponsor. Despite these accusations and increased
regulation by the Vatican, the sisters are hopeful Pope

Francis will focus his efforts on a shared mission: ministering to the poor.

Pope Francis will also need to address the declining numbers of Catholics in some regions. Some church leaders, such as Cardinal Sean O'Malley of the Boston archdiocese, blame the decrease in membership on an increase in secularism in Western societies. The secularism movement looks toward government and other organizations rather than religious groups such as the Catholic Church to shape public policy. Cardinal O'Malley hopes Pope Francis will combat this growing secularism as a way to rebuild the church's influence on societies around the world.

As Pope Francis grows into his role as the leader of the world's largest religion, he and the Roman Catholic Church will face complex challenges. With his strong spiritual foundation and the support of Catholics across the globe, Pope Francis may be able to overcome these challenges and lead the church forward, as he hoped on the night of his election: "And now let us begin this journey, the Bishop and people, this journey of the Church of Rome, which presides in charity over all the Churches, a journey of brotherhood in love, of mutual trust."[12]

TIMELINE

1936
Jorge Mario Bergoglio is born on December 17 in the Flores neighborhood in Buenos Aires, Argentina.

1954
Bergoglio has a revelation during confession in September that prompts him to enter the priesthood.

1958
Bergoglio enters the Society of Jesus on March 11.

1960
On March 12, Bergoglio takes his vows to become a Jesuit; he travels to Chile to study the humanities.

1963
Bergoglio returns to Argentina to study at the Colegio de San José.

1964
Bergoglio becomes a teacher after being turned down for missionary work in Japan.

1969
On December 13, Bergoglio is
ordained as a Jesuit priest.

1973
After less than four years as a priest, Bergoglio
becomes father provincial of the Argentine
province of the Society of Jesus.

1976
On March 29, the Argentine military takes over
the country's government in a coup, starting a
period of violence known as the Dirty War.

1980
Bergoglio takes a teaching position
at the Colegio de San José.

1983
The Dirty War ends when center-left candidate
Raúl Alfonsín is elected president.

1986
Bergoglio travels to Germany for his doctoral studies.

TIMELINE

1992
On May 20, Bergoglio is appointed auxiliary bishop of Buenos Aires by Pope John Paul II.

1993
Bergoglio is named vicar general of the Archdiocese of Buenos Aires on December 21.

1998
Bergoglio becomes archbishop of Buenos Aires on February 28.

2001
Pope John Paul II makes Bergoglio a cardinal; Cardinal Bernard Law of the Archdiocese of Boston, Massachusetts, admits to promoting a priest he knew had sexually abused children.

2006
Despite church opposition, Argentina's Supreme Court votes to allow rape victims the right to an abortion.

2010
Cardinal Bergoglio opposes President Cristina Fernández de Kirchner's bill to legalize same-sex marriage. The bill later passes despite the church's opposition.

2012
In October, the bishops of Argentina make a formal apology to the Argentine people for the church's inability to protect the people from the military dictatorship during the Dirty War.

2013
Pope Benedict XVI resigns as pope on February 11; Pope Francis is elected pope on March 13.

ESSENTIAL FACTS

Date of Birth
December 17, 1936

Place of Birth
Flores, a neighborhood of Buenos Aires, Argentina

Parents
Mario and Regina Bergoglio

Education
University of Buenos Aires; Colegio de San José

Career Highlights
Jorge Bergoglio was ordained as priest in 1969. He became father provincial in 1973. Pope John Paul II named him auxiliary bishop of Buenos Aires in 1992, and Bergoglio took over the role of archbishop of Buenos Aires in 1998 following the death of his predecessor. He began taking on responsibilities in Rome as well as in Argentina when John Paul II made him a cardinal in 2001. Bergoglio was elected pope on March 13, 2013, and took the name Pope Francis.

Societal Contributions

Bergoglio led the Argentine Roman Catholic Church, served as a member of several Vatican committees, and became the first Latin American pope. As a Jesuit, his work focused on improving the lives of the poor and needy in his community.

Conflicts

The role of Bergoglio and of the church during Argentina's Dirty War has proven mysterious and controversial. In the early 2000s, Bergoglio found himself at odds with the increasingly liberal social policies of Argentine presidents. Upon becoming pope in 2013, he inherited the sex abuse and VatiLeaks scandals from his predecessor, Pope Benedict XVI.

Quote

"And now let us begin this journey, the Bishop and people, this journey of the Church of Rome, which presides in charity over all the Churches, a journey of brotherhood in love, of mutual trust." —*Pope Francis*

GLOSSARY

basilica
A large church.

cassock
An ankle-length piece of clothing worn by the pope and other clergy.

clergy
People who are ordained to perform pastoral functions in a Christian church.

coup
A sudden overturning of power, usually by force.

doctrine
A principle of a church.

junta
A group of people holding power after a revolution.

martyred
To be killed for professing a certain faith.

ordained
To be officially made a minister or priest.

Protestantism
A religious movement in the 1500s in which members of the Catholic Church broke away from the church and denied the authority of the pope.

revelation
The communication of a divine truth.

secular
Something not religious in nature.

socialism
A political and economic theory that calls for the means of production to be controlled by the community as a whole.

tenure
A term of office.

theology
The study of religion, God, and God's role in the world.

tumultuous
Marked by upheaval, conflict, and violence.

ADDITIONAL RESOURCES

Selected Bibliography

"Biography of the Holy Father: Francis." *Libreria Editrice Vaticana*. Vatican, n.d. Web. 22 Apr. 2013.

Collins, Michael. *The Vatican*. New York: DK, 2011. Print.

"Pope Francis Biography, Key Facts, Life in Latin America and Background." *Politico*. Associated Press, 13 Mar. 2013. Web. 9 Apr. 2013.

Further Readings

Beller, Susan Provost. *Pope John Paul II and Pope Benedict XVI: Keepers of the Faith*. New York: Franklin Watts, 2007. Print.

Kalman, Bobbie. *Spotlight on Argentina*. New York: Crabtree, 2013. Print.

McDowell, Bart. *Inside the Vatican*. Washington, D.C.: National Geographic, 2009. Print.

Web Sites

To learn more about Pope Francis, visit ABDO Publishing Company online at **www.abdopublishing.com**. Web sites about Pope Francis are featured on our Book Links page. These links are routinely monitored and updated to provide the most current information available.

Places to Visit

Cathedral of the Holy Cross

1400 Washington Street
Boston, MA 02118
617-542-5682
http://www.holycrossboston.com
The Cathedral of the Holy Cross is the main church of the
Roman Catholic Archdiocese of Boston. It was finished in
December 1875 and can seat 1,700 people.

Metropolitan Cathedral

San Martin 27
C1004AAA
Buenos Aires, Argentina
(+54011) 4331 2845
http://www.catedralbuenosaires.org.ar
The Metropolitan Cathedral is the main Catholic church in
Buenos Aires and the previous home church of Pope Francis.
Visitors can take guided tours of the cathedral, the crypt,
and an art exhibition.

Vatican Museums

Viale Vaticano, 00165
Rome, Italy
0039 06 69884676
http://www.museivaticani.va
The Vatican Museums contain art and relics collected over
the past 2,000 years. Visitors can take guided tours or
peruse the museums' collections on their own.

SOURCE NOTES

Chapter 1. Francesco! Francesco!

1. "New Pope 2013, Conclave: White Smoke Signals Cardinals Have Voted." *ABC 15*. Associated Press, 13 Mar. 2013. Web. 2 Apr. 2013.

2. "A Jesuit Pope: Francis." *America: The National Catholic Review*. Catholic News Service, 13 Mar. 2013. Web. 2 Apr. 2013.

3. "Watch Pope Francis Make His First Appearance." *PBS NewsHour*. PBS, 13 Mar. 2013. Web. 2 Apr. 2013.

4. "Roman Catholicism." *Encyclopaedia Britannica*. Encyclopaedia Britannica, 2013. Web. 19 June 2013.

5. "Latin America's Catholics in the Spotlight as Pope Francis Is Installed." *The Pew Forum on Religion and Public Life*. Pew Research Center, 18 Mar. 2013. Web. 27 Mar. 2013.

6. "Transcript: Pope Francis' First Speech as Pontiff." *NPR*. NPR, 13 Mar. 2013. Web. 26 Mar. 2013.

7. Rachel Donadio and Nicholas Kulish. "A Statement Rocks Rome, Then Sends Shockwaves Around the World." *New York Times*. New York Times, 11 Feb. 2013. Web. 26 Mar. 2013.

Chapter 2. Humble Beginnings

1. "Buenos Aires." *Encyclopaedia Britannica*. Encyclopaedia Britannica, 2013. Web. 19 June 2013.

2. Richard Fausset. "Pope Francis' Latin American Upbringing Is Unique Among Popes." *Deseret News*. Deseret News, 23 Mar. 2013. Web. 27 Mar. 2013.

Chapter 3. Building a Spiritual Foundation

1. "Latin America's Catholics in the Spotlight as Pope Francis Is Installed." *The Pew Forum on Religion and Public Life*. Pew Research Center, 18 Mar. 2013. Web. 27 Mar. 2013.

2. "Catholicism in America: Move Over." *Americas View*. Economist, 15 Mar. 2013. Web. 19 June 2013.

Chapter 4. Tumultuous Years

1. Phillip Berryman. *Liberation Theology: The Essential Facts about the Revolutionary Movement in Latin America—and Beyond*. New York: Pantheon Books, 1987. *Google Books*. Web. 19 June 2013.

2. Joseph Ratzinger. "Instruction on Certain Aspects of the 'Theology of Liberation.'" *Congregation for the Doctrine of the Faith*. Vatican, n.d. Web. 21 Apr. 2013.

3. Jim O'Grady. "The Jesuit Background of New Pope Francis." *WNYC News*. WNYC, 14 Mar. 2013. Web. 18 Apr. 2013.

4. "Dirty War." *Encyclopaedia Britannica*. Encyclopaedia Britannica, 2013. Web. 19 June 2013.

Chapter 5. Lowly But Chosen

1. "A Different Option." *Initiation*. San Miguel Schools, n.d. Web. 24 Apr. 2013.

2. "Bishops and Dioceses." *United States Conference of Catholic Bishops*. United States Conference of Catholic Bishops, 2013. Web. 19 June 2013.

3. Anthony Faiola. "Jorge Mario Bergoglio, Now Pope Francis, Known for Simplicity and Conservatism." *Washington Post*. Washington Post, 13 Mar. 2013. Web. 9 Apr. 2013.

4. Ibid.

5. "Argentine Bishops Apologize for Failings during Military Rule." *Today's Top Stories*. Catholic World News, 13 Nov. 2012. Web. 24 Apr. 2013

6. "A Renewed Culture of Life and Family—Appeal from Cardinal Jorge Mario Bergoglio." *L'Osservatore Romano*. Vatican, 21 Jul. 2011. Web. 7 May 2013.

Chapter 6. Tiny Nation, Largest Religion

1. "St. Peter's Square." *Saint Peter's Basilica*. Vatican, n.d. Web. 25 Apr. 2013.

2. "Saint Peter the Apostle." *Encyclopaedia Britannica*. Encyclopaedia Britannica, 2013. Web. 19 June 2013.

Chapter 7. A Spiritual Philosophy

1. Anthony Faiola. "Jorge Mario Bergoglio, Now Pope Francis, Known for Simplicity and Conservatism." *Washington Post*. Washington Post, 13 Mar. 2013. Web. 9 Apr. 2013.

2. "Pope Francis: From the End of the Earth to Rome." New York: Harper, 2013. *Google Books*. Web. 19 June 2013.

3. Laurie Goodstein. "New Pope Puts Spotlight on Jesuits, an Influential Yet Self-Effacing Order." *New York Times*. New York Times, 16 Mar. 2013. Web. 9 Apr. 2013.

SOURCE NOTES CONTINUED

Chapter 8. Looking Toward the Future

1. Laura Smith-Spark, Richard Allen Greene, and Michael Martinez. "New Pope Talks Courage on First Day." *CNN.* CNN, 14 Mar. 2013. Web. 27 Apr. 2013.

2. Rachel Donadio and Nicholas Kulish. "A Statement Rocks Rome, Then Sends Shockwaves around the World." *New York Times.* New York Times, 11 Feb. 2013. Web. 26 Mar. 2013.

3. Miranda Leitsinger. "'Woefully Inadequate' or a 'Great Reformer': Child Sex Abuse Crisis Overshadows Benedict's Legacy." *US News.* NBC News, 11 Feb. 2013. Web. 22 Apr. 2013.

4. "Vatican Sets Record Straight on Sexual Abuse." *Catholic Education Resource Center.* Catholic Education Resource Center, 22 Sept. 2009. Web. 19 June 2013.

5. Philip Pullella. "Pope Francis Urges Decisive Action Against Sex Abuse." *Reuters.* Reuters, 5 Apr. 2013. Web. 27 Apr. 2013.

6. Miranda Leitsinger. "'Woefully Inadequate' or a 'Great Reformer': Child Sex Abuse Crisis Overshadows Benedict's Legacy." *US News.* NBC News, 11 Feb. 2013. Web. 22 Apr. 2013.

7. Rachel Donadio and Jim Yardley. "Vatican's Bureaucracy Tests Even the Infallible." *New York Times.* New York Times, 18 Mar. 2013. Web. 20 June 2013.

8. Ibid.

9. Laurie Goodstein and Megan Thee-Brenan. "US Catholics in Poll See a Church Out of Touch." *New York Times.* New York Times, 5 Mar. 2013. Web. 20 June 2013.

10. Nicole Winfield. "Pope Francis Supports Crackdown on US Nuns." *Associated Press.* Associated Press, 15 Apr. 2013. Web. 20 June 2013.

11. Laurie Goodstein and Megan Thee-Brenan. "US Catholics in Poll See a Church Out of Touch." *New York Times.* New York Times, 5 Mar. 2013. Web. 20 June 2013.

12. "Transcript: Pope Francis' First Speech as Pontiff." *NPR.* NPR, 13 Mar. 2013. Web. 26 Mar. 2013.

INDEX

INDEX CONTINUED

ABOUT THE AUTHOR

Amanda Lanser is a freelance writer who lives in Minneapolis, Minnesota. She and her husband are animal lovers and have two cats, Quigley and Aveh, and a greyhound, Laila. Amanda enjoys writing books for kids of all ages, and she hopes to visit the Vatican someday.

ABOUT THE CONSULTANT

Dr. Massimo Faggioli is an assistant professor of theology at the University of Saint Thomas in Saint Paul, Minnesota. He received his PhD from the University of Turin in Turin, Italy, in 2002. He is a researcher, author, and lecturer on such topics as the history of Christianity, the Second Vatican Council, and the new Catholic movements. Among his books are *Vatican II: The Battle for Meaning* (2012; translated in Italian and Portuguese) and *True Reform: Liturgy and Ecclesiology in Sacrosanctum Concilium* (2012, translated in Italian).